Finding Out for Yourself

SCIENCE PROJECTS: 3

"Finding out for yourself is often the best way to learn." With that statement, William Moore sums up the philosophy and purpose of this book. The author leads young scientists into a variety of investigations, offering suggestions to assist the student in conducting his own methods of gathering information, reaching conclusions, and displaying his work in a meaningful visual form.

Finding Out for Yourself

SCIENCE PROJECTS: 3

by William Moore

G. P. Putnam's Sons  New York

FOUNDED 1838

GPPS

Contents

1494494

HOW TO USE THIS BOOK

This book is about animals and plants and about the many changes that are taking place in everything around you. It will help you investigate or poke into things you may be curious about. Finding out for yourself is often the best way to learn. Scientists do this all the time.

After looking through the book, you may want to choose one or more projects to work on. If so, you can just follow the suggestions until you have a science project of your own. Of course, you don't have to follow the suggestions exactly as they are given. You can change them if you wish. You may also find that you can use the ideas in this book for looking into something that is not included as one of the projects in this book. The main thing, whatever you decide to do, is to find out for yourself.

1. PETS

If you have ever had a pet, you know that it can be great fun. People have always had pets. Even thousands and thousands of years ago when men lived in caves, they had dogs for pets. The dogs lived with the people in the caves, kept them warm at night, helped them hunt for food, and warned them of danger. Most of the animals we keep as pets today had ancestors that lived long before men appeared on earth. Dogs, horses, birds, and other animals lived millions of years before man. You can learn much about animals from your pet.

This big fellow owns the author's family. His name is Brownie. His mother was a Doberman, and his father was a Boxer. He grew to be about 20 inches high at the shoulder and weighs more than 60 pounds. He is tall like a Doberman, but heavy like a Boxer.

About Your Dog

1. Give him a private place to eat and sleep. A dog needs a place he can call his own.
2. Give him something safe to chew on, such as a hard rubber bone.
3. Brush and comb him every day.
4. If he is five weeks to five months old, feed him four times each day. If he is five months to eight months old, feed him three times per day. If he is more than eight months old, feed him one meal a day.
5. Don't give him chicken bones, fish bones, or fried foods.
6. Feed him at the same time each day and remove what is left after forty-five minutes.
7. Don't scold or punish him for doing something after he has done it. You must catch him in the act.
8. If you brush him regularly, you will need to bathe him only once or twice a year.
9. Take him to a veterinarian for advice on feeding and for his shots to prevent distemper and rabies.

This is Queenie. Jimmy's pet is almost full-grown. She will not grow much larger than she is now. How do we know that puppies and children, too, will grow only to be so large or so tall?

9

1. How long do dogs live?
2. How can you teach a dog?
3. How fast will he grow?
4. What may make him sick?
5. In what ways are dogs like people?
6. In what ways have dogs helped people?
7. Do dogs need people?

FINDING ANSWERS TO YOUR QUESTIONS

1. Ask your parents and friends about dogs they have owned. Take notes on what you learn from them.

The girl is Kathleen. The dog is Brownie. The girl is three years old and will not reach her full height for another ten years or more. The dog is one year old and is as tall as he will ever be. Different kinds of animals, as well as plants, grow at different rates.

2. Buy a booklet from a pet store and copy those parts that answer your questions.
3. Visit a veterinarian or pet doctor. Write some of his answers in your notebook.
4. Look for books about dogs in your neighborhood and school libraries. Take your notebook with you and copy the information you need.
5. If possible, visit an obedience or training school for dogs. Write what you learn.

USING YOUR ANSWERS TO MAKE A SCIENCE PROJECT

1. Find a large piece of cardboard or ask an older person to cut a piece from a carton.
2. Paint, crayon, or use colored tape to make a border around the edges of the cardboard.
3. Paste or tape a photograph of your dog to the cardboard. If you do not have a dog, use a picture from a magazine.
4. Write the answers to your questions neatly on a clean sheet of paper. On another sheet of paper, write where you looked and where you found the information.
5. Fasten these sheets to the large cardboard.
6. In an empty space on the cardboard, print a title for the project, such as "How Long Dogs Live" or "How To Teach a Dog."

About Your Cat

1. When selecting a new pet, try to choose one that is at least six to nine weeks old.
2. Give it a warm, cozy place in which to sleep.
3. Give it two saucers: one for food, and one for milk or water.
4. Place a plastic litter pan in one spot where the kitten can always find it. This will be its toilet.
5. Gently comb and brush your pet daily.
6. While your kitten is six weeks to three months old, feed it four times each day and be sure the food is at room temperature. When the pet is three months old, feed it only three times daily. When it reaches five months, give it only two meals per day. At six months of age, offer it only one meal a day plus a bowl of milk.

This is Jim-Jim, a Siamese cat. Like most other Siamese cats, he meows or makes other noises much of the time. Some cats do not meow often. Cats are also different in color markings, size, length of tail, length of fur, color of eyes, and in the things they like to do.

7. Consult your local pet store or an animal doctor about the kinds and amounts of food.

8. Do not feed your pet spicy foods, lamb chops, or chicken bones.

9. Take your kitten to an animal doctor for shots to prevent feline distemper. An animal doctor or veterinarian can also help cure your kitten of any other illness.

1. What can you and what can't you teach a cat?
2. How fast does a kitten gain in weight?
3. How long do cats live?
4. What causes a cat to be sick?
5. In what ways are cats like (and unlike) people?
6. What kinds of cats are not kept as pets?

FINDING ANSWERS TO YOUR QUESTIONS

1. Write in a notebook what you have learned from your own cat.
2. Ask your parents and friends about cats they have owned. Write what you learn from them in your notebook.
3. Visit a pet store that sells kittens and buy a booklet about them. Write in your notebook the answers you found in the booklet.
4. Ask a veterinarian or pet doctor the questions you wish answered. Write his answers in your notebook.
5. Look for books and magazines about kittens in your neighborhood or school library. Take your notebook with you.
6. Ask your parents if you could visit someone who raises pedigreed kittens. Write what you learn in your notebook.

14

1. Find a large piece of cardboard or ask an older person to cut a piece from a carton.
2. Fasten one or two snapshots of your pet to the cardboard. If you do not have a kitten, cut a picture of one from a magazine.
3. Use colored tape, paint, or crayon to make a border around the cardboard.
4. Write the answers to your questions on a sheet of clean paper and fasten it to the cardboard.
5. On a separate sheet of paper, write a list of the places where you looked and found information. Fasten this sheet to the cardboard.
6. In an empty space on the cardboard, print your name and the questions you have answered.

About Your Canary

HOW TO CARE FOR YOUR CANARY

1. You will need the following equipment:
   a. cage
   b. cage cover (to protect your pet from air currents and noise)
   c. paper (to cover the bottom of the cage)
   d. canary seed (the daily food for your bird)
   e. cuttlebone (this contains calcium, which birds need)
   f. special "song food" (helps the bird to sing)
   g. birdbath (to hold bath water)
   h. treat cup (for song food and biscuit)
   i. egg biscuit (a special dessert)
   j. white grit with charcoal (for bottom of the cage)
2. Be sure your pet and cage are kept in a quiet part of the home where there are no drafts of air.
3. Consult an expert about the food needs and illnesses of your canary.

This is not a canary! Can you figure out what kind of bird it is? This is a baby goose, or goose chick, which could very well become someone's pet. Many kinds of birds are kept as pets.

Courtesy of the American Museum of Natural History

1. How long do canaries live?
2. What can canaries learn?
3. What can cause a canary to become sick?
4. How do canaries differ from one another?
5. In what ways are canaries like other birds or unlike other birds?
6. In what ways are canaries like people?

FINDING ANSWERS TO YOUR QUESTIONS

1. If you have owned a canary, write what you have learned in a notebook.
2. Ask any relative or friend who has owned a canary.
3. Get a booklet about canaries from a pet store.
4. If possible, talk to an expert who has raised or bred canaries.
5. Visit a zoo or a museum that exhibits birds.
6. Look for books or articles about canaries in your school or neighborhood library. Take your notebook along.
7. Ask a veterinarian or pet doctor who knows about birds. Write what you have learned in your notebook.

1. Find a cardboard carton and have an older person cut a large, rectangular piece from it for display purposes.
2. Use colored tape, crayon, or paint to make a border around the edge of the cardboard.
3. Find pictures of canaries in magazines. Cut them out neatly and paste them on the cardboard. Good pictures may be found in magazines that can be bought in pet shops. Print a title or caption under each picture.
4. Write all of the answers to your questions on one piece of paper. Place a title at the top of the paper and your name at the bottom.
5. On a separate sheet of paper, carefully list all of the places you looked for or found answers to your questions.
6. Fasten both sheets of paper to the large sheet of cardboard.
7. In an empty space on the cardboard, print the title of your project. Choose a title such as "What Can Canaries Learn?"

About Your Hamster

1. The box or cage which will be his home should be at least one square foot in size. A hamster needs this much space to move about and exercise. A glass aquarium makes a good home, too.
2. Keep him where the temperature will not go below 50 degrees or above 80 degrees.
3. Place a removable pan in the bottom of his cage and cover it with strips of newspaper, sawdust, or wood chips.
4. Clean his cage at least once a week.
5. You can give him a block of wood to gnaw on, as well as a slide, an exercise wheel, and a ladder.
6. Play with him gently, a little bit each day. Hamsters have very poor vision at close range. Pick him up gently from the back of the neck so he is not frightened by the sight of a hand he cannot recognize.
7. The word "hamster" comes from the German word *hamstern,* which means hoarder in English. Adequate amounts of food are necessary to satisfy his hoarding instinct. Feed him either once or twice each day and give him all he wants to eat. Getting fat will not hurt him.

8. A grown hamster can eat prepared pellet food, dog biscuits, vegetables, fruits, grains, and nuts. In winter, mix four drops of cod-liver oil with his food. Be sure he has a supply of fresh water.

9. Try not to wake him until the afternoon. He will sleep most of day and stay up most of the night.

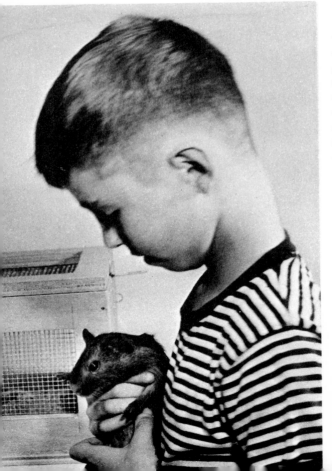

This is Jonathan Moore with his pet. The cage shown here is lined with one-quarter-inch wire screen and has a clean-out drawer. Both guinea pigs and hamsters can be purchased at many pet stores.

1. How many things can a hamster be taught to do?
2. In how many ways are hamsters like guinea pigs?
3. In what ways can hamsters get hurt or become ill?
4. How have hamsters been used by scientists?
5. How do wild hamsters live and take care of themselves?
6. How do hamsters differ from one another?
7. In what countries do wild hamsters live?
8. In what ways are hamsters like and unlike squirrels?
9. What animals are the enemies of hamsters?

A guinea pig grows to be about 6 inches long. He has four toes on each front leg and three toes on each hind leg. Scientists have used guinea pigs and hamsters for many experiments, but hamsters are more popular as pets.

Courtesy of the American Museum of Natural History

FINDING ANSWERS TO YOUR QUESTIONS

1. If it is helpful, write in a notebook what you have learned from your own pet.
2. Ask a science teacher where you can find information about hamsters and guinea pigs.
3. Visit your school or neighborhood library and look through the catalogue cards for books and articles about hamsters. Take your notebook with you.
4. Visit any zoo or museum that exhibits small animals such as hamsters. Take your notebook along.
5. A pet store may have a booklet containing information about hamsters.
6. If possible, ask your doctor for information about the value of hamsters and guinea pigs to medical research.
7. A veterinarian or pet doctor may also have information about hamsters and guinea pigs. Write what is helpful in your notebook.

USING YOUR ANSWERS TO MAKE A SCIENCE PROJECT

1. If you own a hamster or a guinea pig, you can exhibit him as a part of your project. If you do not have such a pet, pictures of one mounted on a piece of cardboard or construction paper will serve the same purpose.

2. Write on a sheet of paper what you think are the correct answers to your questions. Also tell why you think your answers are correct.
3. On a separate sheet of paper, list all the things you have done and the places you have looked for information. Include the titles of books. Be sure to sign your name and class to both sheets of paper.
4. Fasten both sheets of paper to the cardboard or construction paper.
5. You may use a question you have answered as a title. Print it at the top of the cardboard or construction paper.

About Your Mouse

1. A glass tank is an excellent home for mice, since it is easy to clean and makes it easy for you to see through the glass sides.
2. Cover the bottom of the tank or cage with sawdust. Place a small wooden box inside for nesting, and some absorbent cotton for the mice to use in building a nest. You will also need two tiny containers, one for water and one for food.
3. You can feed mice oats, dog biscuits, mixed birdseed, hay, bits of bread soaked in milk or water, and fresh vegetables. An adult mouse will eat a teaspoon of oats or seed and a teaspoon of wet bread each day.
4. In order to keep their teeth in good condition, you should give your pets a small piece of beef bone to gnaw on. You can try walnuts and acorns, too.

24

5. Don't give your mice bacon and cheese. These foods are very fattening and are not part of their natural diet.
6. Since mice are very active animals, you can give them a tiny ladder, a swing, and a sliding board to play on.

This wild mouse is called the white-footed mouse. It has crawled out of its winter home deep in the earth to search for food. Wild mice do not make good pets. Mice that do make good pets are those that had grandparents which were house mice.

Courtesy of the American Museum of Natural History

1. What can mice be taught to do?
2. How long do mice live?
3. What can cause mice to become ill?
4. How do scientists use mice?
5. Which animals are natural friends and which are natural enemies of mice?
6. In what ways are mice different from cats?

These baby white-footed mice are one day old. Born in a bale of cotton, they are not yet strong enough to stand on their feet. Not even their ears will stand up.

Courtesy of the American Museum of Natural History

1. You may find the answers to your questions by studying your own pet. Write what you learn in a notebook.
2. Ask any friends and relatives who may have owned mice.
3. Visit your public library or school library and look for articles in books and magazines about mice. Take your notebook with you.
4. Get a booklet about mice from your local pet store.
5. Visit a museum or zoo that exhibits mice or other rodents. Be sure to take your notebook and pencil with you.
6. Ask a veterinarian or pet doctor for information about mice. Write his answers in your notebook.
7. Ask your science teacher where you might find answers to your questions.

USING YOUR ANSWERS TO MAKE A SCIENCE PROJECT

1. If possible, display your pet mice in their tank or cage. Be sure to attach a card on which you have written your name and the names of your pets and any other information you wish.
2. If you do not own such pets, fasten photographs or pictures cut from magazines to a large sheet of cardboard.

27

3. Use paints or crayons to make a border around the cardboard.
4. Write on a sheet of paper what you think are the correct answers to your questions, and tell why you think the answers are correct. Sign your name to the paper, too.
5. On a separate sheet of paper, list all the places you have looked and found answers to your questions. Include dates, addresses, and titles, wherever possible.
6. Attach both sheets of paper to the large piece of cardboard.
7. If it is helpful, also fasten samples of food and other materials to the cardboard.
8. In an empty area of the cardboard, print the name of the project.

About Your Turtle

1. If your turtle is a small one, keep him in a small plastic bowl. If your turtle is a large one, you may need an aquarium.
2. The water must be deep enough for him to swim. Provide a dry, raised surface on which he can sit and dry off.
3. If any rocks are used, be sure they have no edges sharp enough to cut your pet.
4. Your turtle does not need sunlight, but the light from a 50- to 100-watt bulb will give him enough warmth. Be sure the bulb is placed about ten inches above the turtle, and leave it on for about eight hours each day.
5. Keep the temperature in the bowl between 60 and 80 degrees, and do not completely cover the opening.
6. Feed your turtle only once every two or three days. If necessary, a turtle can go for about a month without eating. Consult your local pet store or buy a booklet on turtles for information about food.

7. Feed him in a separate pan at mealtime. Wash the pan with soap and water after each feeding.
8. Wash the turtle bowl or tank at least once each week with soap and water.
9. Consult a pet store booklet or a book from the library about illness or the things which may hurt a turtle.

On a warm summer day you may, if you are careful, see dozens of these fellows sunning themselves on logs and rocks in the middle of a pond. They will slip into the water quickly, however, as you approach. This one is a baby painted turtle and is found almost everywhere.

QUESTIONS TO ASK YOURSELF

1. How long do turtles live?
2. What can a turtle learn?
3. How fast and how large can a turtle grow?
4. How well do turtles hear, smell, and see?
5. In what ways are turtles like and unlike other animals?
6. How are turtles different from one another?

FINDING ANSWERS TO YOUR QUESTIONS

1. Examine your own turtle or one owned by a friend. Write what you have learned in a notebook.

Here is a closeup view of a painted turtle. It is dark olive-brown on top, with some green or yellow around the edges. At the very edge of the shell are bright red spots. Underneath, the turtle is a bright lemon yellow.

Courtesy of the American Museum of Natural History

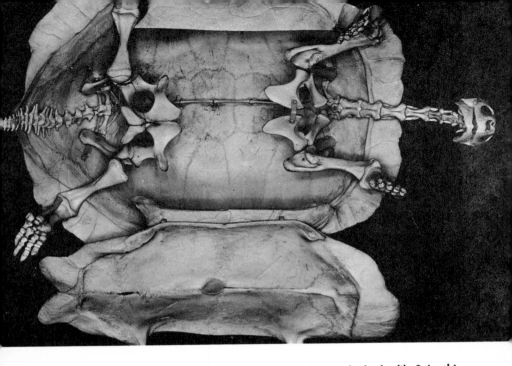

Have you ever wondered what the inside of a turtle looks like? In this view, everything has been removed except the skeleton. The turtle is on his back, and the bottom shell has been swung aside so that the inside and the bones can be seen.

2. Talk to any relative or friend who may have owned a turtle. Ask them for information which may help to answer your questions.

3. Buy a booklet about turtles and copy any important information it may contain.

4. Visit a museum or zoo that has specimens of turtles. Take your notebook and pencil along with you.

5. Look for books and magazine articles abut turtles in your school or neighborhood library. Write what you learn in your notebook.
6. Men who go fishing sometimes catch turtles. If you know a fisherman, ask him about turtles. Write his answers in your notebook.
7. Ask your science teacher where you might find information about turtles.

USING YOUR ANSWERS TO MAKE A SCIENCE PROJECT

1. Display your own bowl or tank with your turtle in it. Be sure to attach a small piece of paper with your name, as well as the turtle's name, on it.
2. If you do not have a turtle, display a picture of one cut from a magazine.
3. Display any booklet or magazine that contains information about turtles.
4. On a sheet of paper, write what you think are the correct answers to your questions. Be sure to sign your name to the paper.
5. On a separate sheet of paper, list all the places you visited and the books or articles you have read. Sign your name to this paper and display both pieces of paper.
6. If you have any other pictures of turtles, mount them on a piece of cardboard and display them.

About Your Frog or Toad

HOW TO CARE FOR A FROG OR TOAD

1. Frogs and toads lay eggs, which grow into tadpoles; then the tadpoles grow into frogs or toads. If you have tadpoles, ask your pet store owner about food called *Infusoria* and *Elodea*. When the tadpoles lose their tails and become true frogs or toads, you can feed them all kinds of small worms. Some types of frogs and toads will eat insects and small minnows or darters.

2. You'll need a fairly large tank or aquarium as a home for your pet. The tank has to have water as well as dry land or rocks so your pet can be in the water or out of the water as he chooses.

3. If it gets too cold in your tank, your pet will try to hibernate (which means he will try to go underground to keep warm). Either a light bulb near the tank or an aquarium heater (from your pet store) will prevent him from getting too cold.

This is a very young tadpole. Instead of a mouth, it has a sucking mechanism which helps fasten the tadpole to plants and rocks in the water.

Courtesy of the American Museum of Natural History

The pickerel frog is found all over North America. He spends most of his time in the water. He can grow to be about 4 inches long. This one has his head above water so he can breathe and look about.

1494494

QUESTIONS TO ASK YOURSELF

1. What is the difference between frogs and toads?
2. How and why do frogs croak or sing?
3. Do frogs or toads cause warts to grow on people?
4. What can cause a frog or toad to become sick?

5. What does the word "amphibian" mean, and what animals can be called by this name?
6. What can you teach a frog or toad to do?
7. How are frogs or toads like or unlike people?
8. How do frogs find their own food?

FINDING ANSWERS TO YOUR QUESTIONS

1. Use a notebook to record what you learn from your toad or frog. Be sure to include your pet's name, age, size, markings, and food.
2. Talk to friends or relatives who have owned or observed frogs and toads.
3. Take your notebook to a school or neighborhood library and write information you find in books and magazines.
4. Get a booklet about frogs and toads from a pet shop.
5. Visit a zoo or museum that exhibits such animals.
6. Talk to a veterinarian or pet doctor and ask for answers to your questions.
7. Ask adults who go fishing in, or who have lived around, lakes and ponds.
8. Talk to a science teacher who may know where to find more information about frogs and toads.

1. If possible, display your frog or toad in his tank. Be sure to attach a card on which you have written your pet's name and age, your own name, and any other information you wish to add.

2. If you do not own a frog or toad, fasten a photograph or picture cut from a magazine to a large sheet of cardboard. Have an adult help you cut out such a piece of cardboard from a carton.

3. Paint, crayon, or tape a border around the edges of the cardboard.

4. Write what you think are the correct answers to your questions, and why you think they are correct, on a sheet of paper. Sign your name to this sheet.

5. On a separate sheet of paper, list all of the places where you have looked for answers and where you have found answers. Include dates, addresses, and titles.

6. Attach both sheets of paper to the large sheet of cardboard.

7. Also, if necessary, include samples of food and other materials used in finding the answers to your questions.

About Your Chameleon

1. A terrarium is simply a place to keep land animals. It is similar to an aquarium, except that it contains soil instead of water. A glass terrarium is easy to clean and allows your chameleon to get plenty of light. You can also watch your pet easily in a glass terrarium. A fish tank makes a good terrarium when a screen is fitted tightly over the top. A wide-mouthed gallon bottle with several holes punched in the lid will also make a good terrarium. Place less than an inch of white sand or gravel in the bottom. On top of the sand, place a twig or branch for climbing and a small broad-leafed houseplant or two.

2. You can feed your pet small crickets, grasshoppers, houseflies, fruit flies, mosquitoes, caterpillars, grubs, mealworms, or tiny bits of meat. Some chameleons can be taught to eat from the hand of their owner.

3. Place a small piece of fresh fruit in the box or terrarium where he lives. The fruit will attract flies and other insects, which the chameleon will capture in his mouth and eat.

38

4. Let your pet get his water from a few drops sprinkled daily on the plant leaves in his terrarium. Most chameleons will ignore water placed in a dish.
5. The temperature of the terrarium must be kept between 50 and 90 degrees. The terrarium may be kept in a sunny place and a 40-watt light bulb may be used at night, when necessary, to keep the temperature from going below 50 degrees.
6. A booklet on chameleons can be found at your local pet store or in some libraries. It will give you additional information about caring for your pet.

Can you find the chameleon? It can stay like this, with its head downward, for a long time. By remaining absolutely motionless, it can escape detection by its enemies.

Courtesy of the American Museum of Natural History

1. What can a chameleon learn?
2. What can cause a chameleon to become sick?
3. What causes a chameleon to change color?
4. In what ways are chameleons like or unlike alligators?
5. Which animals are enemies of chameleons?
6. How can you breed chameleons?

FINDING ANSWERS TO YOUR QUESTIONS

1. Study your own chameleon and write what you have learned in a notebook.
2. Ask friends or relatives who have owned a chameleon and write their answers in your notebook.
3. Secure a booklet about chameleons from your local pet shop.
4. Look for books and articles about chameleons in your school and neighborhood libraries.
5. Visit a museum or zoo where lizards are exhibited. Take along your notebook.
6. If possible, ask a veterinarian about chameleons and other cold-blooded animals. Record his answers in your notebook.

1. If possible, display your chameleon in his terrarium. Be sure to attach a card on which you have written your own name, as well as your pet's name, along with his age and any other information you wish to add.

2. If you do not own a chameleon, paste a picture of one on a large sheet of cardboard.

3. Write what you think are the correct answers to your questions on a sheet of paper and attach it to the cardboard.

4. On a separate sheet of paper, list all of the places where you have looked for or found answers to your questions. Fasten this sheet to the large piece of cardboard.

5. Print the title of the project, as well as your name, on the cardboard. A question you have selected may very well serve as a title.

About Your Rabbit

1. A rabbit home is called a hutch. You may keep a rabbit outdoors or indoors. If the hutch is outdoors, it can be made of wire-mesh screen and wood. It should be at least 2 feet deep by 4½ feet long and 2½ feet high, and about one-third of this space should be closed in with wood or canvas to serve as a bedroom. The entire hutch should be about two feet off the ground and placed so that it is not in the sun for long periods.
2. Use hay, straw, or peat moss for bedding.
3. The entire hutch should be cleaned at least once each week.
4. Feed your pet twice a day. Give him a morning meal of grains and cereals, and an evening meal of greens such as cabbage leaves, spinach, beet tops, clover, and dandelion leaves. Be sure to wash the greens before feeding.
5. Provide a dish of clean water and some thick, green twigs to chew on. You can also use rabbit pellets and some hay for roughage. Rabbit pellets can be purchased at the pet store.
6. Plenty of exercise is good for your pet. You can even walk him on a harness and leash.

Notice the tail on this rabbit. The little white tail gives him the name cottontail. For a pet, however, you will want a domesticated rabbit— one that will live contentedly in a cage and can be taken care of.

1. How long do rabbits live?
2. What can you teach a rabbit?
3. What can cause a rabbit to become sick?
4. How many kinds of rabbits exist and how do they differ?
5. How are rabbits different from people?
6. Can rabbits become friendly with cats and dogs?
7. What animals are the natural enemies of rabbits?

Here is a nest of six young rabbits. How many can you find in the picture? The rabbits are protected by living in a hole in the ground and by the grass and weeds that usually cover the hole.

Courtesy of the American Museum of Natural History

1. Some answers to your questions may be found by studying your own pet. Write what you have learned in a notebook.
2. Talk to friends and relatives who may have owned a rabbit.
3. Ask your parents if you can visit someone who raises rabbits. Take your notebook along.
4. Get a booklet about rabbits at your local pet store.
5. Take your notebook and visit your public, neighborhood, or school library and look for books and articles about rabbits.
6. Visit a museum or zoo that exhibits such animals. Take your notebook with you.
7. Get what information you can from a veterinarian or pet doctor.
8. Ask a science teacher where you can find more information about rabbits.

USING YOUR ANSWERS TO MAKE A SCIENCE PROJECT

1. Find a large sheet of cardboard or have someone help you cut one from a carton.
2. Mount some photographs of your pet, or pictures of rabbits cut from magazines, on the large sheet of cardboard.

3. Use paints, crayons, or colored tape to make a border around the edges of the cardboard.
4. On a sheet of paper write what you think are the correct answers to your questions, and why you think they are correct. Sign your name to this paper and attach it to the cardboard.
5. On a separate sheet of paper, list all of the places you have looked for information about rabbits. Include dates, addresses, and titles where possible. Fasten this sheet to the cardboard display sheet.
6. In an empty space on the cardboard, print the title of the project and your name.

2. COLLECTIONS

You can become an expert on almost anything you decide to collect. Being an expert means that you will know more about something than most other people. Many of the world's scientists have been or are collectors. By collecting things, you can see a larger number of them than most people do. You can compare things and see the differences among them. By arranging and rearranging the things you have collected, you can also see many more ways in which they are alike as well as unlike. Collecting things also helps you to get rid of false or untrue ideas you may have had.

A large collection is often better than a small one because you can learn more from a large one. Collections make very good science projects. You may never have thought of it, but a zoo is a collection. It is a collection of animals, displayed so that everyone can learn about animals. Museums also have collections. You can learn much about collecting by visiting a zoo or a museum.

Collecting Leaves

Spring moves north, at about fifteen miles each day, until it finally reaches your neighborhood. Spring is a good time to look for small buds which will become leaves. It is a good time to start your collection. In the winter, of course, you can collect the leaves of houseplants or of flowers or of vines that have kept their leaves.

The numbered leaves may be identified as follows:

1 quaking aspen; 2 redbud; 3 sassafras; 4 catalpa; 5 balm of Gilead; 6 swamp cottonwood; 7 linden; 8 hazelnut; 9 southern cottonwood; 10 black willow; 11 willow oak; 12 narrow-leaved cottonwood; 13 wax myrtle; 14 red cherry; 15 papaw; 16 sugar maple; 17 sycamore; 18 tulip tree; 19 sweet gum; 20 silver poplar; 21 American elm; 22 sweet cherry; 23 water elm; 24 tupelo; 25 red plum; 26 serviceberry; 27 chestnut; 28 chestnut oak; 29 beech; 30 holly; 31 Osage orange; 32 cottonwood; 33 white birch; 34 Lombardy poplar.

Courtesy of the American Museum of Natural History

The numbered leaves, all of which are compound leaves, may be identified as follows:

1 white ash; 2 pumpkin ash; 3 black, or water ash; 4 mountain ash; 5 red ash; 6 prickly ash; 7 box elder; 8 hop tree; 9 Kentucky coffee tree; 10 Hercules'-Club; 11 horse chestnut; 12 Ohio buckeye; 13 yellowwood; 14 shagbark hickory; 15 bitternut; 16 pignut; 17 mockernut; 18 pale hickory; 19 smallfruited hickory; 20 pecan; 21 butternut; 22 black walnut; 23 yellow buckeye; 24 honey locust; 25 common locust.

1. How many different shapes of tree leaves can be found in your neighborhood?
2. How do the sizes of tree leaves differ in your neighborhood?
3. How long does it take a bud to become a full leaf?
4. What can cause a leaf to become unhealthy?
5. How different are the leaves of the different kinds of oaks or maple trees?
6. How different are the leaves of fruit trees from those of shade trees?
7. How much alike and how much different are the leaves of flowers?
8. How do the leaves of vines differ from each other?
9. How are the leaves of hedges like and unlike the leaves of trees?
10. Do trees, hedges, vines, and rosebushes lose their leaves at the same time or at different times?

FINDING ANSWERS TO YOUR QUESTIONS

1. Observe the trees and plants in your own yard or neighborhood. Use a notebook to record what you have seen.
2. Collect specimens from plants and trees in your own neighborhood. Be sure to ask permission before doing so.

3. Visit a public park. Observe trees and other plants. Collect leaves only if they are on the ground. Take your notebook with you.
4. Take your notebook along when you go on a picnic or a drive through a rural area.
5. Get someone to take you to any botanic garden that you can. Again, be sure to take your notebook with you. A camera can also be used to record facts about leaves.
6. There are books and magazines in both your school and public library which will be helpful.
7. Some museums may exhibit plants along with their leaves. Be sure to take your notebook and a pencil along.

USING YOUR ANSWERS TO MAKE A SCIENCE PROJECT

1. As you collect leaves, you can save them for display by pressing them between the pages of an old telephone book.
2. You can preserve leaves by dipping them in a shallow pan of melted paraffin. Dip them quickly for a light coat of paraffin.
3. It is easy to make plaster of Paris casts of your leaves. The plaster can be purchased at drugstores and craft shops. Add small amounts of water and a few drops of vinegar to a batch of plaster until

it becomes a paste. Put a small quantity of plaster in the center of each leaf and gently push it toward the edges. Be sure the plaster is of uniform thickness before it hardens.

4. A plaque can be made of plaster by using a small, shallow paper plate or pan. Fill the pan with plaster paste and then gently press the leaf into the smooth surface of the plaster. Lift the leaf out

You can mix plaster of Paris with water in a can. Pour the wet plaster into a small pie plate, and before it hardens press your leaf into the plaster.

After removing the leaf, allow time for the plaster to harden. Then you can paint the plaster.

carefully. Use watercolors to paint either the impression or the surrounding area.

5. Write what you think are the correct answers to the questions you have selected. Explain why you think they are the correct answers.

6. On a separate sheet of paper, list the places where you have looked for and found specimens.

7. Display both pieces of paper and your leaves. Display also a card on which you have printed the name of your project, as well as your own name and class.

Collecting Seeds

Have you ever wondered how many different kinds of plants there are in the world? Everywhere you go, you will find new kinds of plants. They grow from seeds, of course. Inside each seed is a tiny plant. This tiny plant, inside a seed, is a remarkable thing. A plant inside a seed may be able to live there for several years. It often can survive extreme heat and extreme cold. Once you put it in soil or in water and keep it warm, however, the plant inside begins to grow. Some plants grow quickly from seeds, while others grow slowly. You can conduct some exciting experiments with seeds once you have started your collection.

These buckeyes, as they are called, are the seeds of the horse-chestnut tree. The buckeye forms inside a hard shell. The outer shell shown here has been sawed open so its thickness can be seen.

1. How long does it takes a seed to grow into a plant which can be seen?
2. How long does it take a seed to grow into a plant which produces seeds?
3. What seeds are eaten as food?
4. How do seeds travel some distance from the plant on which they grow?
5. How many different sizes and shapes of seeds can be found in one neighborhood?
6. What conditions are necessary for a seed to grow into a healthy plant?
7. Where do seeds appear on flowers?
8. How can new plants be made to grow without using seeds?
9. How many seeds are produced by a single plant?
10. Do little seeds grow into little plants and big seeds into big plants?

FINDING ANSWERS TO YOUR QUESTIONS

1. If possible, collect seeds from the plants (including trees) in your own yard or neighborhood.
2. Buy packets of flower and vegetable seeds at stores that sell them.

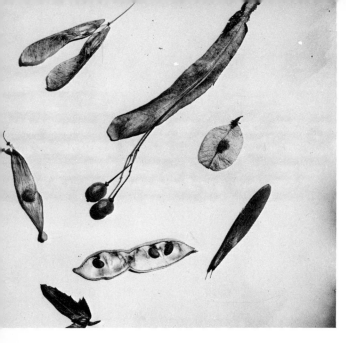

Pictured are the fruits of seven trees: linden, elm, ash, black locust, maple, ailanthus, and hornbeam.

3. Visit a greenhouse and ask for seeds of plants to add to your collection.
4. If you live on a farm or can visit one, you will find many seeds there.
5. The grocery store is a good place to look for seeds and fruits containing seeds.
6. Your local newspaper will sometimes carry advertisements of companies that sell seeds. Write to them.
7. In your own school or public library, you will find books and articles about plants and seeds. Ask the librarian to help you.

8. Ask your parents where you can get a seed catalogue.
9. Ask your teacher where you can find additional information about seeds.

USING YOUR ANSWERS TO MAKE A SCIENCE PROJECT

1. Display your seeds cemented or taped to a large sheet of cardboard or on the lid of a cardboard box.
2. Print a number and the name of each seed underneath it. Add any other information you think will be interesting.
3. If you have experimented with growing seeds, display the plants you have grown.
4. On a piece of paper, write what you think are the correct answers to the questions you have selected. Write also why you think they are the correct answers.
5. On a separate sheet of paper, list all the places you have looked and found both seeds and answers to your questions. Include dates, addresses, and any titles.
6. Decorate your cardboard or box lid with paints or crayon.
7. Be sure to print the title of the project and your name and class on the lid or cardboard.

Collecting Shells

If you live near the ocean or some other large body of water, you can collect shells. These are the hard, bony parts of animals that live in the water. Some shells give the animal protection from other animals and help to keep it alive, while other shells merely serve to stiffen the animal as our skeleton does. You can learn much about animals that live in the sea by collecting their shells.

This is a scallop shell. Shells of this type are especially interesting because of their colors and fanlike shapes.

Courtesy of the American Museum of Natural History

1. How can you tell the age of the animal that lived in a shell?
2. How do animals with shells move about?
3. How do the enemies of such animals attack them?
4. How are oyster shells used to help grow more oysters?
5. How do some animals use their shells to destroy wooden ships and the piles of docks and wharves?
6. Where do jingle shells come from?
7. What are pen shells, and where do they come from?
8. How do shells help make pearls?
9. How can you identify clam, oyster, mussel, and other common shells?
10. How do barnacles use their shells to protect themselves?

FINDING ANSWERS TO YOUR QUESTIONS

1. If you live near an ocean or other large body of water, collect a few shells which are as undamaged or unbroken as possible.
2. If a friend or relative goes on a trip or vacation near a beach, ask him to collect shells for you.

3. Visit a museum where shells are displayed. Take your notebook with you and write the names of a few of them. Draw pictures, too, if you can.
4. Ask your parents to buy some animals with shells at a fish market. Use the shells from these animals as a part of your collection.
5. At your school or public library, look for books on sea life and animals. Take your notebook along with you.

USING YOUR ANSWERS TO MAKE A SCIENCE PROJECT

1. Cover the bottom of a small box with cotton and place each shell in a separate spot. Paste a small card to the cotton under each shell. Number the shells by writing numbers on the cards.
2. Attach a large card to the box or its lid, and on the card print the number and name of each shell.
3. Write what you think are the correct answers to your questions and why they are correct on a sheet of paper. Sign your name to the paper.
4. On a separate sheet of paper, list all of the places you have looked and found either shells or the answers to your questions.
5. If you wish, paint or crayon the box and display your two papers with it.

lava

gneiss   slate

mica-schist   granite

marble   quartzite

Courtesy of the American Museum of Natural History

Collecting Rocks

From rocks, scientists have learned much about the age of the earth and what has happened to it over the years. Scientists have read the story of what the earth was like before there were people. They have learned about plants and animals that lived long ago, and they have learned why many no longer exist. From rocks, they have learned how ice covered parts of the earth, how mountains were formed, how oceans changed, and how volcanoes erupted. You can learn much from the rocks in your own neighborhood.

1. How many different kinds of rocks can be found in your neighborhood?
2. Why do some rocks show layers of different colors?
3. Why are some rocks soft and others hard?
4. Why are rocks of different colors?
5. How do rocks become sand?
6. Why can fossils, the remains of plants and animals, be found inside rocks?
7. How do fossils become changed into rocks?
8. Of what are rocks made?
9. Why are some rocks smooth and round?
10. How can you tell which rocks contain copper, iron, or other metals?

FINDING ANSWERS TO YOUR QUESTIONS

1. With an older person, explore the shore of a nearby ocean, lake, or river. Take a small bag with you in which to carry your collection.
2. A gravel pile, a gravel driveway, or an unpaved country road are good places to look for rocks.
3. If you live near a rock quarry, you can easily find specimens there.
4. If you live near a place where gravestones are pre-

pared for a cemetery, you can ask for small pieces of these stones for your collection.

5. If you have a backyard or live on a farm, you may find many stones either at or near the surface. You can dig most of them out.

6. Observe the stones that are used in some buildings. Use your notebook to write about the appearances of these stones. Note their color, hardness, size, and smoothness or roughness.

7. Visit a museum where rocks are displayed. Take your notebook along and write in it the names of some of the rocks and what they are like.

Any box can be fixed up like this cigar box for displaying a collection of rocks. The protractor with the weighted string can be used to note the angle of rock layers while collecting. Partitions can be made from other boxes and glued into place. Paper with adhesive backing was used to cover the box in the picture.

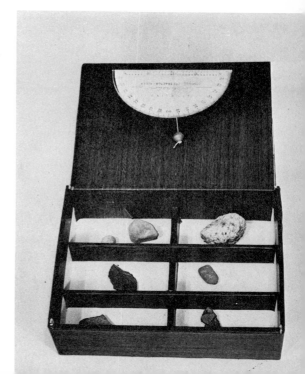

8. At your local public or school library, you can find books and articles about rocks. Use your notebook to record interesting information.
9. Art museums and stores that sell stone to sculptors may also be places to look for information.

USING YOUR ANSWERS TO MAKE A SCIENCE PROJECT

1. You can cement your collection to a piece of stiff cardboard or place them in plaster of Paris while it is still soft.
2. Number each rock, and after learning the names by comparing them with pictures in a book about rocks, write the names on a separate card or in a special area on the cardboard.
3. Write what you think are the correct answers to your questions on a piece of paper. Also tell why you think they are the correct answers.
4. Make a list of all the places you have looked for and found rocks and the answers to your questions about rocks. Include the dates and addresses, as well as the titles of books you have read.
5. Paint, crayon, or use colored tape to make a border around the cardboard.
6. Be sure to print the title of the project, as well as your name and class, on the cardboard.

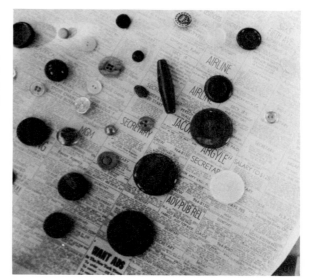

Shown in this picture are just a few of the many kinds of common buttons.

Collecting Buttons

Buttons are interesting for many reasons. They are made in different sizes, shapes, colors, and designs. They are also made of different materials and come from many different parts of the world. The story of buttons is part of the story of how man has clothed himself and of how he has made practical and artistic use of many materials around him. You can learn much about man and his use of materials just by collecting buttons.

1. Of what materials are most buttons made?
2. How many different materials are used?
3. Why are some materials better than others?
4. In what ways are some modern buttons better than those made long ago?
5. In how many ways are buttons used for decorative purposes and not as fasteners?
6. In what ways are some buttons made more attractive than others?
7. Do people all over the world use the same kinds of buttons?
8. In how many ways are buttons attached to clothing?
9. What kinds of fasteners are taking the place of buttons and why?
10. From what parts of the earth do button materials come?

FINDING ANSWERS TO YOUR QUESTIONS

1. Ask your mother or any other woman who sews if she has a button box or a sewing box in which buttons are saved. You may start your collection with some of these.

2. Ask for the buttons from old or worn-out clothing. Save them in a box.
3. If possible, buy some interesting buttons at a store.
4. Ask your friends and relatives for any buttons that might interest you.
5. Attics and basements sometimes contain trunks and boxes of old clothing from which you may collect some interesting buttons.
6. Write to companies that make buttons and ask for information about them.
7. Look in sewing magazines for pictures and information about buttons.
8. Visit your local public and school libraries. Ask the librarian about books that contain pictures and information about the clothing worn in various periods of history and in various countries of the world. Take your notebook along with you.

USING YOUR ANSWERS TO MAKE A SCIENCE PROJECT

1. Ask for help in getting a large sheet of cardboard on which to mount your buttons.
2. Arrange your buttons several times in several different orders until you are sure the collction shows what you want it to show. Then use glue or cement to fasten the buttons to the cardboard.

3. Print neatly under each button the name of the material it is made of and whatever else you think is important.
4. On a sheet of paper, write what you think are the correct answers to your questions and why you think they are the correct answers.
5. On another sheet of paper, list all of the places you have looked for and found answers. Be sure to include the dates, addresses, and titles so that other people can use this information.
6. Print the title of the project on the cardboard along with your name and class.
7. Use crayon, paints, or colored tape to make a border around the cardboard.

3. CHANGES

Scientists believe that everything moves and everything changes. Movement and change are a part of our lives and of everything around us. We are even changed by the things we learn. Learning to read or to roller-skate changes us and makes us a little bit different from what we were before.

We know that day changes into night, summer into winter, seeds into plants, and boys and girls into men and women. We may not be so aware, however, that nonliving things also change. Water changes into ice, rocks into sand, iron into rust, wood into smoke and ashes, a liquid perfume into air, and electricity into light or heat. Did you know that distance and move· ment change things, too? A motion-picture projector changes stationary pictures on a film into moving pictures. Airplanes have changed the time it takes to go long distances. Objects a long way off look a great deal smaller than they do when we are close to them.

Scientists have always been concerned about change. You will often find that changes are important as well as interesting.

The movement of water is causing rocks to change into pebbles and sand. The pebbles and sand, in turn, are moved by the action of the water.

Liquids Change by Evaporation

After a shower or rain, you have seen the sidewalks and streets dry up. Perhaps you already know that this happens more rapidly when there is warm sunshine and the wind is blowing. The liquid water changes into a gas and disappears into the air. This process is called evaporation. You have also seen the water on a washed blackboard evaporate into the air. At home, perhaps, you have noticed that a liquid perfume changes into a gas which you cannot see—but which you can detect with your nose. Puddles of water, ponds, lakes, rivers, and oceans also lose water by evaporation. Scientists have learned much about the earth by studying evaporation. You may find investigating this kind of change a worthwhile study.

On a sunny day the heat of the sun may turn much of the water in this river to a gas, which may then become clouds. Some evaporation goes on even when there is no sun.

U.S. Forest Service

1. How much does sunshine help evaporation?
2. How does moving air or the wind help evaporation?
3. Which will evaporate faster, alcohol or water?

FINDING ANSWERS TO YOUR QUESTIONS

1. a. Use two cups that are exactly alike. Fill them with exactly the same amount of water.
   b. On a sunny day, place one cup in the sunshine and the other cup in a shady spot. Make sure that both are either exposed to the wind or are protected from the wind.
   c. Write in your notebook the exact time you placed the cups in position, how much water was in the cups, and if it was a windy day or not.
   d. Look at both cups every two or three hours until you have noticed any difference in the amounts of water. Mark the levels of water with a marking pen or pencil.
2. a. Pour equal amounts of water into two cups that are exactly alike. Do this on a dry, warm day, rather than a wet, cold one. Mark the levels.
   b. Place one cup in a room where there is no draft or wind. Place the other cup on the sill of an open window. Be sure that both cups are not in the sunshine at any time.

c. Look at the cups every two or three hours. Mark the changes in water level with a pencil.

d. Write in your notebook the exact time you placed the cups in position. Write also the exact time you inspected the cups and what differences you found in water levels.

3. a. Ask your parents for an exact thimbleful of alcohol. Pour the alcohol into a clean, dry saucer. Do the same with a thimbleful of water, using another saucer.

   b. Place both saucers near each other.

   c. Look at the saucers frequently. Write in your notebook the exact time you placed the saucers in position and the exact time each became dry.

USING YOUR ANSWERS TO MAKE A SCIENCE PROJECT

1. Display the saucers or cups or anything else you have used in the experiment.

2. On a small card, print the title of the experiment and your name. The title might be "Evaporation Experiment."

3. On a clean sheet of paper, write the title. Underneath it write the questions you tried to answer. Then write what you think are the correct answers and why. Tell what you did to find the answers. Include dates and times.

These objects, which once were quite useful, have lost much of their value due to rusting. What could have been done to prevent the materials from becoming rusty?

Iron Changes by Rusting

Metals that have iron in them will rust. Rust is the reddish-brown material which forms on metals that have iron in them. One way to tell if a metal has iron in it is to look for rust spots. Another way to tell if a metal has iron in it is to test it with a magnet. If a magnet is attracted to the metal, you will know that it has iron in it. You may have seen a pair of roller skates that have been left outdoors for a few days and nights and noticed the rust spots on them. Perhaps you have noticed rusty nails. Things that have a lot of iron in them will sometimes rust completely away so that there is nothing left but rust. Other metals also change in the same way. Rust is the name we give to this new material when it forms on iron.

1. How many small objects found around the house contain iron?

2. How much does water help in causing rust?

FINDING ANSWERS TO YOUR QUESTIONS

1. a. Collect some small objects such as a paper clip, a nail, a coin, a key, a ring, a pencil with a metal band around it, a spoon, and a screw.

   b. Place each of these things in a separate cup or glass of water and allow them to stay there for two or three days.

   c. Look for some reddish-brown material on these things and in the water.

   d. If you are still not sure, test the objects with a magnet. Objects containing iron will be attracted to the magnet.

2. a. Get a half dozen new nails, paper clips, or other metal objects. Test them with a magnet to make sure they contain iron.

   b. Make sure two of them are completely dry. Be sure there is no moisture on your hands when handling them. Place them in a dry place such as a drawer.

75

c. Place two of them where only damp air will touch them. This could could be on a porch, in a garage, or on a windowsill. Make sure that no rain or water touches them.

d. Place two of them in a glass of water.

e. Leave all six of them in place for three or four days before examining them. Compare the amount of rust that appears on the pairs of objects.

USING YOUR ANSWERS TO MAKE A SCIENCE PROJECT

1. Attach the objects to the lid of a cardboard box. You can punch holes in the lid and tie them on, or you can use cement.

2. Print a title such as "Rusting Is a Change" at the top of the lid. Print your name at the bottom of the lid.

3. On a sheet of paper write exactly what you did in trying to find answers. Be sure to write your name and class at the bottom of this sheet.

The Changing Seasons

Spring, summer, fall, and winter: these are the changes that take place every year. Even though the calendar may say that spring comes on March 21, it may not arrive exactly on that day. It is not a sudden change. Spring comes north at a speed of about fifteen miles each day. Later, spring will turn into fall at about the same speed. Spring is a time when the coldness of winter changes to the warmth and wetness of spring. Ice melts; earth and growing things begin to thaw. You can tell when spring is beginning to arrive: the tiny, hard buds on the tree branches begin to soften and swell. Then the outer scales of the buds open. Tender little leaves appear.

Of course, not only leaves appear in the spring. Some buds begin to turn into flowers, and new plants push their way up out of the wet soil. The changes are everywhere. People change the kind of clothing they wear, some birds fly north, and animals come out of the places they have been sleeping all winter. The changing seasons change the life of all living things. Just as interesting are the changes that take place in nonliving things. The rocks, the rivers, the oceans—all things on the surface of the earth—change with the seasons. Scientists are still learning about these changes.

Look for the rabbit tracks. You can follow them with your eyes for many yards through the woods.

Courtesy of the American Museum of Natural History

The woods in summer is dense with leaves, and you cannot see far into the woods. Even if there were rabbit tracks in the earth, you could not follow them easily. Fishing is fun, however, during any season.

1. What happens inside a plant when spring comes?
2. What changes do the seasons make in the lives of boys and girls?

FINDING ANSWERS TO YOUR QUESTIONS

1. a. Cut off two stalks of celery with leaves on them.
   b. Pour water into two cups until they are half full. Add a little blue ink so that the water in both cups is blue.
   c. Place one cup in the refrigerator with the cut end of the celery in the blue water.
   d. Place the other cup on a windowsill in the warm sunshine. Put the other celery stalk in this cup.
   e. After several hours, take the celery out of the refrigerator and compare it with the one left in the sunshine. What differences do you see?
2. a. Use four pages in your notebook. At the top of each page, write the name of a season.
   b. Do the games and sports you play change with the seasons? Write on the proper page the games you play in each season.
   c. How does your clothing change? Write the names of the clothing you wear that is different for each season.

d. Does the food you eat change with the seasons? Write these changes on the proper pages.

e. Does the amount of time you spend indoors and outdoors change with the seasons? If so, estimate the amount of time you spend outdoors and put this information on the proper pages.

f. Write on the proper pages any other changes you think are interesting or important.

USING YOUR ANSWERS TO MAKE A SCIENCE PROJECT

1. Use sheets of colored construction paper or a large sheet of cardboard. For the celery stalk experiment, draw or crayon pictures of the celery and the cups on the paper. For the notes you took for each season, cut pictures out of old magazines and paste them on the paper or cardboard. Pictures of clothing, food, and games are not hard to find. Print a title under each picture.

2. On a sheet of writing paper, neatly write what you think are the correct answers and why you think they are correct.

3. On a separate sheet of paper, list exactly what you did, step by step.

4. Fasten both sheets of paper to the cardboard or to one of the sheets of colored construction paper.

Freezing and Melting Are Changes

Have you ever seen a liquid change to a solid, or a solid change to a liquid? We all have, of course. We have seen water freeze into solid ice and ice melt into water. We know that a change in temperature can cause these things to happen. Changes in temperature can cause many other things to change, too. Scientists have learned much about the earth by studying how liquids change to solids and solids to liquids. You will find, that freezing and melting make interesting experiments.

A lake can be fun in both summer and winter. Fishing is a popular sport during the summer.

Bureau of Reclamation, Boise, Idaho

Some people also enjoy fishing through the ice during winter months. Ice may form several feet thick on a lake, and the melting process can take weeks in the springtime.

1. How long does it take a cup of water to become solid ice in your refrigerator?
2. How long does it take an ice cube to melt completely?

FINDING ANSWERS TO YOUR QUESTIONS

1. a. Place a cup of water in the freezing compartment of your refrigerator. Also place a thermometer next to it. Write in your notebook the exact time you placed them in position.
   b. Check the cup of water every ten minutes until ice begins to form. After ice begins to form, check it regularly by picking up the cup and tipping it. Do not push your finger into the cup. You will be able to see if there is still liquid water under the ice just by tipping the cup. Write in your notebook the exact time at which all the water was frozen solid.

2. a. Use three ice cubes that are almost exactly the same size. Place each in a separate cup. Place one cup in the part of the refrigerator where milk and fruit juice are kept. Place one on a table in the middle of a room. Place the third cup on a radiator or sunny windowsill.

b. Write the exact time you placed the cups in position in your notebook. Inspect each cup every five minutes. Write in your notebook the exact time each cube changed completely to a liquid.

USING YOUR ANSWERS TO MAKE A SCIENCE PROJECT

1. On a sheet of paper, write exactly what you did, step by step. Include the time, the temperature, and the kind of cups you used. Write also what you think are the correct answers to your questions and why you think they are correct. Sign your name at the bottom.
2. On a separate sheet of paper, draw a picture of the cups and the thermometer. Number or letter each cup in the picture and underneath print the minutes or hours it was used. Print your own name and class at the bottom.

Burning Is a Change

Man has always known that fire changes things. A forest fire destroys an entire forest, changing beautiful trees to charcoal, ashes, and smoke. Fire can also change a ship, a home, an automobile, or airplane so that they are no longer useful. People can be hurt by being burned, but people are often helped by fire. One kind of burning keeps us warm and cooks our food, and another kind makes our automobiles and airplanes run. The sunshine that warms our earth and helps plants to grow comes from a kind of burning on the sun. Scientists have learned much about the earth and about life on the earth by studying the burning process. You can also learn some interesting things by finding out what scientists already know about burning.

An entire forest was changed by a fire as beautiful trees became charcoal and ashes. Burning often causes a rapid change in many things. What other changes will take place because these trees were destroyed?

Courtesy of the American Museum of Natural History

1. How did the Indians start fires?
2. What burns inside an automobile engine, a diesel engine, a jet airplane engine, and your home furnace?

FINDING ANSWERS TO YOUR QUESTIONS

1. a. Look for books and articles in your school and public libraries.
   b. Look in an encyclopedia for fire-making methods used by primitive peoples. Copy the important information in your notebook.
   c. Talk to a Boy Scout or his troop leader about places you can look for information.
   d. Visit a museum that displays Indian crafts and skills.

2. a. Look in a good dictionary or an encyclopedia. Use your notebook to record the facts.
   b. Visit your school library or the local public library and ask for magazines about automobiles, airplanes, diesel trains and tractors, and also home heating.
   c. Ask an automobile mechanic or a furnace repairman to explain how engines and furnaces operate.

1. Collect old magazines from friends and relatives. Cut out pictures of Indians and fire-making or of engines and furnaces.
2. Paste your pictures to a large sheet of cardboard. Print a title at the top of the cardboard.
3. Use paint, crayon, or tape to make a border around the cardboard.
4. On a sheet of paper, write what you think are the correct answers to your questions and why you think they are correct. Also list the places you have looked and found answers to your questions.
5. Fasten this sheet of paper to the large cardboard. Be sure to print your name and class at the bottom.

Decaying Is a Change

Living things decay. Leaves, twigs, bark of trees, and insects all die and fall to the ground. On the ground, they become broken into many small pieces and turn a dark color. Farmers and gardeners call this material humus. Humus is good for young plants, since humus contains much plant food. Decaying is a change by which living things become food for newer living things. You can experiment with humus yourself.

The ground is covered with leaves, twigs, bark, dead insects, and other material. All of these will become broken into smaller pieces and decay. A farmer or gardener calls such decayed material humus.

1. How helpful is humus to growing plants?
2. How many different things can be found in humus?

FINDING ANSWERS TO YOUR QUESTIONS

1. a. If possible in the late fall, cut two small, young branches from a tree and plant them deep in the ground several feet apart. Make sure both branches are the same thickness and length. Build a short fence around one of the branches. This can be made with sticks of wood driven into the ground or with wire. Fill the fenced area around the branch with humus. Do not put humus around the other branch.

   b. In the spring, note which branch has more buds and leaves and grows faster.

   c. If you cannot plant things in the ground, experiment in the same way with a flower box or clay pots.

2. a. If possible, examine some humus yourself. See how many different plant or animal parts you can recognize. In your notebook, write the names of those you can identify.

   b. Ask a gardener or a farmer about the living things that decay and change into humus. Write his answers in your notebook.

89

1. Make a collection of some of the living things that will decay and become humus. A leaf, a twig, a piece of bark, and even a dead insect may be used.

2. Cut from old magazines pictures of living things that most often decay and are used as humus.

3. Fasten your pictures or your specimens of living things to the lid of a large cardboard box. Use transparent tape or cement. Name each item and print your name and class on the cardboard.

4. Place some dry humus in a cigar box or some other small container. Paste a cover of colored paper on the box. Print the words "Sample of Humus" on the lid. Add your name and class.

5. Write on a sheet of paper what you think are the correct answers to your questions and why they are correct. List all of the things you did to find the answers.

6. Attach this sheet of paper to the cardboard lid.

Growing Is a Change

Some things change quickly. You can watch them change. The weather often changes in a few hours. Ice melts quickly in a warm place. A piece of paper will change to ashes and smoke in a few seconds. Growing, however, is often a slow change. Some plants take weeks or even months to grow enough for us to see the changes. People grow slowly, too. You know that it usually takes sixteen to eighteen years for many people to reach their full height and weight. Scientists have learned much from studying how people grow and the different speeds at which their heights and weights change. You will find growth an interesting kind of change to investigate.

The fish in the boy's hand have grown to full size in a few months. The boy is ten years old, but he has not reached his full size. In about how many more years will he be grown to his full height? Do boys always become as tall as their fathers?

1. Do animals grow at different speeds?
2. In addition to growing taller, how many other ways do plants grow?

FINDING ANSWERS TO YOUR QUESTIONS

1. a. Find out at what ages a cat, a dog, and a horse reach their full size. Use encyclopedias and other books in your school or public library. Take your notebook with you.

   b. Ask your parents how tall they expect you to be when you have reached your full height. Compare your present height to this expected height. Write in your notebook what fraction of the expected height you have reached.

2. a. Look carefully at a very young tree. Estimate its height, its thickness of trunk, the number of branches, and leaves.

   b. Look at an older, fully grown tree of the same kind. Estimate the height, trunk thickness, number of branches, and leaves.

   c. Find a book on trees in your school or public library. Discover how the root system changes as the tree grows. Draw a picture of the root system of a tree.

1. Find pictures of trees or animals in old magazines. Cut out the ones you wish to use and mount them on a large sheet of colored construction paper. Print the names of the trees or animals underneath each picture. Also print ages or growth records if you have this information.

2. On a sheet of writing paper, write what you think are the correct answers and why you think they are correct. Be sure to title the page and also sign your name and class.

3. On a separate sheet of paper, list all of the places you have looked for information and which were the most useful. Print a title, such as "Sources of Information," and also sign your name.

4. If the sheet of construction paper is large enough, fasten both sheets of writing paper to it with staples or other fasteners.

Glossary

amphibian—a cold-blooded animal, such as a frog, toad, or salamander, that lives part of its life in the water and part on land.

ancestor—a person from whom one is descended distantly.

aquarium—a glass container for water in which animals may live.

botanic garden—a garden in which one can study plant life.

decay—a process by which a dead plant slowly loses its identity.

diesel—a kind of engine in which fuel oil is burned or exploded simply by being compressed.

distemper—an infectious disease of young dogs caused by a virus.

estimate—to make an approximate judgment or measurement.

evaporation—the process by which a liquid changes to a vapor or gas.

experiment—a step which is taken or a procedure which is followed for the purpose of discovering something unknown.

feline—any member of the cat family.

fossil—any remains or trace of an animal or plant of long ago.

greenhouse—a glass house for raising and protecting tender plants.

hibernate—to sleep or spend a long period of time in close quarters.

hoarder—one who collects or accumulates things for future use.

humus—decayed material that forms part of the soil.

litter—the babies born to an animal; also, chopped-up material for animal use.

paraffin—a white or colorless waxy substance, used for making candles and waterproof coatings.

pedigreed—an animal whose parents and ancestors are known because their identities have been recorded.

plaster of Paris—a white, powdery material that swells when mixed with water and then hardens rapidly.

rabies—an infection of the brain caused by a virus.

rust—a reddish material which forms on the surface of iron and metals containing iron.

specimen—a single example or part of a larger group or number; also, a typical part or member of a large mass of things.

terrarium—a container, usually made of glass, in which land animals and plants can be raised.

veterinarian—a person able to treat animals that are sick or injured.

Index

The Author

William Moore is a teacher of industrial arts in the public schools of New York City. Building on his interest in science, which dates back to his school days, he continues to help young people with school and home science projects. In addition, Mr. Moore has become well-known for his magazine articles in the fields of woodwork, metalcraft, and how-to-do-its of all kinds. Mr. Moore is a graduate of Ohio State University. He and his family live in Brooklyn, New York.